EXPLORING

GREAT INVENTIONS

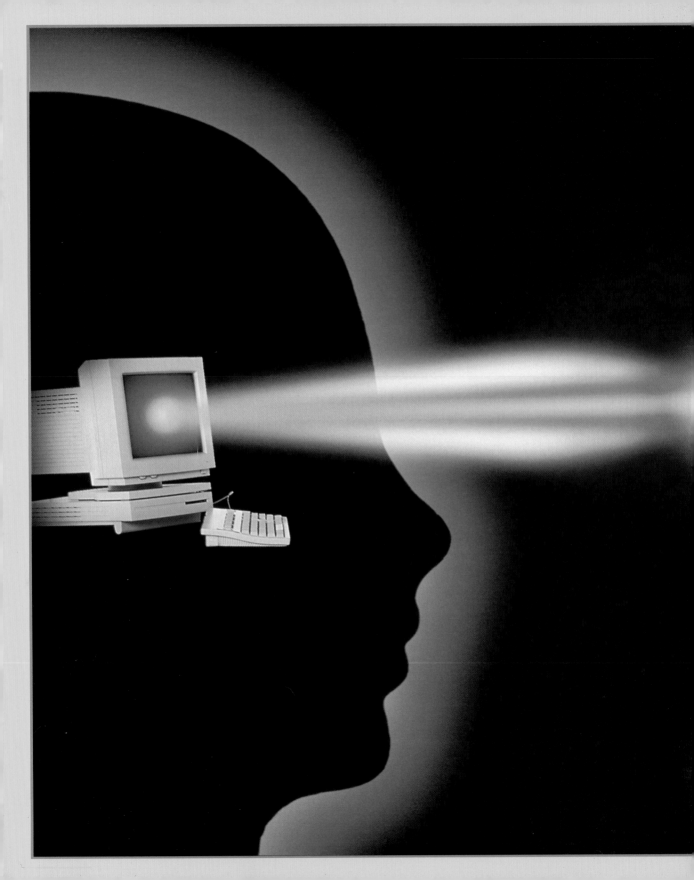

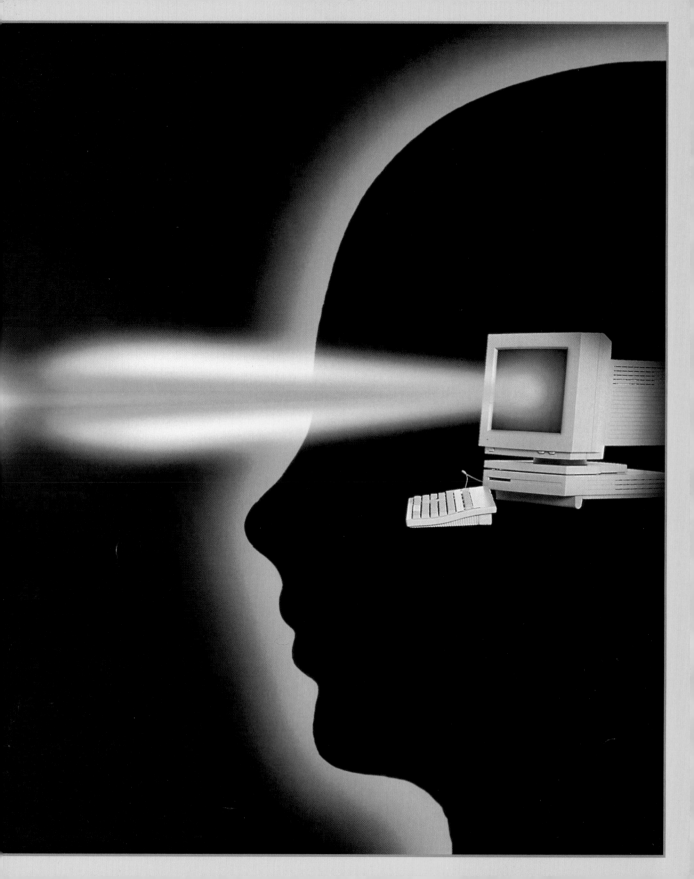

Photo Credits:
AP/Wide World Photos—Cover; Pages 6-11, 13-19, 21-29
Corbis-Bettman—Pages 12-13, 16, 18, 25
Gamma Liaison—Pages 15, 19
Bill Debold/Gamma Liaison— Page 12
Jonathan Kirn/Gamma Liaison—Pages 26-27
Sam Sargen/Gamma Liaison—Page 19
Richard Shock/Gamma Liaison—Page 27
Roger Viollet/Gamma Liaison—Page 26
The Granger Collection—Pages 6-8, 10, 14, 16, 18, 20-21, 26
Mike Agliolo/International Stock—Cover; Endpages; Pages 7, 21, 23, 28
Wayne Aldridge/International Stock—Page 20
George Ancona/International Stock—Cover
Azzato/International Stock—Page 23
I. Wilson Baker/International Stock—Page 27
John Bechtol/International Stock—Cover
Jim Cambon/International Stock—Page 13
Ken Frick/International Stock—Page 12
Michael Manheim/International Stock—Page 11
John Michael/International Stock—Pages 12-13
Noble Stock/International Stock—Page 18
Tom O'Brien/International Stock—Page 8
Orion/International Stock—Page 6
Dario Perla/International Stock—Cover
Stockman/International Stock—Page 11
Johnny Stockshooter/International Stock—Page 21

Eyes on Adventure

Exploring

Great Inventions

Written by
Philip Koslow

kidsbooks®
Incorporated

This eleven-year-old invented a music stand called the "Flip-O-Matic." It allows musicians to turn a page of sheet music with their foot.

WHAT IF?

Inventions are usually born when someone ponders a problem and comes up with a solution. These creative leaps of imagination have enabled humans to change the world in very exciting ways.

▲ ROUND AND ROUND

Where would we be without the wheel? It may well be the most important invention in history because it has been used to perform so many different tasks, from grinding grain to driving machinery. Solid wooden cart wheels and potter's wheels were used in Mesopotamia (present–day Iraq) after 4000 B.C.

FORGING AHEAD ▶

Fire was not "invented," but people had to learn how to put it to good use. One of its most important uses was extracting iron from rocks. With iron tools, people cleared forests and created large, permanent communities.

POWERFUL POWDER

Some of the earliest inventions were weapons. Gunpowder, which greatly changed the nature of warfare, was first used by the Chinese around A.D. 850 for fireworks. In the 13th century, Europeans began using gunpowder to fire cannons and guns.

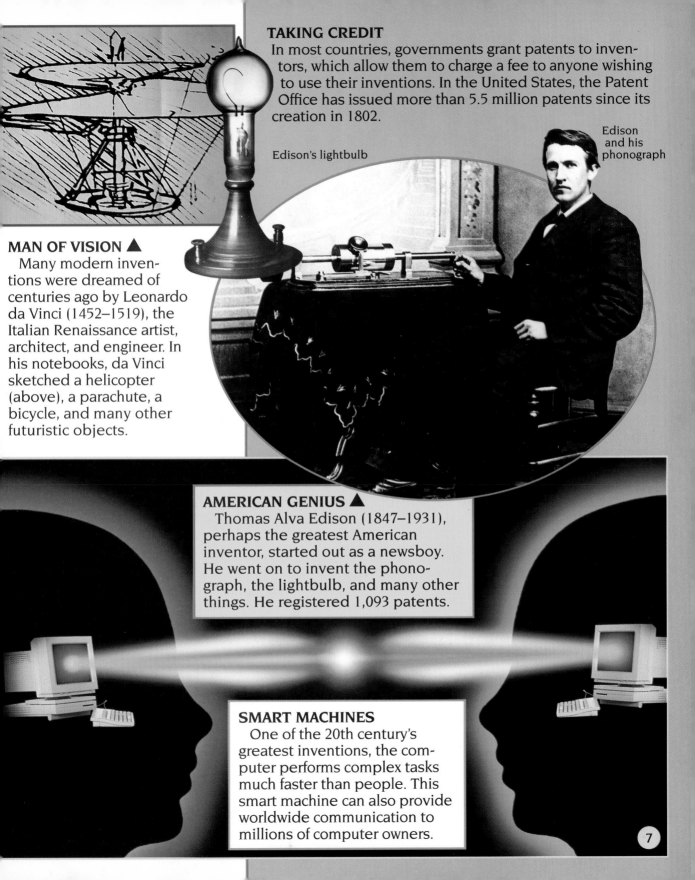

TAKING CREDIT

In most countries, governments grant patents to inventors, which allow them to charge a fee to anyone wishing to use their inventions. In the United States, the Patent Office has issued more than 5.5 million patents since its creation in 1802.

Edison and his phonograph

Edison's lightbulb

MAN OF VISION ▲

Many modern inventions were dreamed of centuries ago by Leonardo da Vinci (1452–1519), the Italian Renaissance artist, architect, and engineer. In his notebooks, da Vinci sketched a helicopter (above), a parachute, a bicycle, and many other futuristic objects.

AMERICAN GENIUS ▲

Thomas Alva Edison (1847–1931), perhaps the greatest American inventor, started out as a newsboy. He went on to invent the phonograph, the lightbulb, and many other things. He registered 1,093 patents.

SMART MACHINES

One of the 20th century's greatest inventions, the computer performs complex tasks much faster than people. This smart machine can also provide worldwide communication to millions of computer owners.

TURNING ON THE JUICE

Long ago, people relied on their own muscle power to make things work. In time, they learned to use the strength of animals they managed to tame. Finally, they devised ways to tap Earth's resources, a quest that is still continuing.

GUSHER ▶

The first oil well in the United States was sunk in Pennsylvania in 1859, by Colonel Edward L. Drake. From crude oil came gasoline, which spurred the development of the internal combustion engine and became the source of power for cars and planes.

◀ CHARGED UP

In 1752, Benjamin Franklin made one of the earliest demonstrations of electricity. By flying a specially rigged kite during a thunderstorm, Franklin was able to attract an electric charge from the atmosphere. He used this experiment to invent the lightning rod, which has since saved many homes.

One of the first steam-powered locomotives was invented by Nicholas Cugnot in France in 1769.

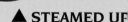

▲ STEAMED UP

After many improvements on the steam engine, the Age of Steam was born in the late 18th century. In England, Edmund Cartwright created the first steam–powered automatic loom in 1787. This invention kicked off the Industrial Revolution, replacing skilled handworkers with armies of laborers who operated machines in giant factories.

BLOW BY BLOW

Vertical windmills —used to harness the power of the wind for grinding grain—were invented in England during the late 12th century. Today, giant windmills help create electricity.

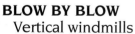

Hoover Dam provides enough power to serve 1.3 million people in Nevada, Arizona, and California.

ATOMS FOR PEACE

After scientists unleashed the frightful power of the atom bomb in 1945, they worked to find positive uses for nuclear energy. In 1954, the Soviet Union built the first nuclear reactor designed to generate electricity.

WATER POWER

The use of water power to create electricity began in 1882, when a *hydroelectric* power station opened on the Fox River in Wisconsin. The station was able to provide an electric current for two paper mills and a private home.

Often used in demolition, dynamite brought down this 31-story hotel.

ZAP!

A laser beam can reach 11,000°F and cut through steel and diamonds. It can be focused so accurately that it could heat a pot of coffee 1,000 miles away! The first laser, a device using the energy created by microwave radiation, was produced by the American physicist Theodore Maiman in 1960. Lasers have many applications. This police officer uses a less intense laser beam to determine the speed of a passing car.

BOOM!

During the 1860s, Alfred Nobel found a way to stabilize the explosive called nitroglycerin. He called his invention *dynamite* after the Greek word dynamis, which means "power." Nobel then used the wealth he earned from dynamite to create the Nobel Prizes.

9

MIGHTY MACHINES

From the simplest devices, such as levers and pulleys, to the combustion engine, machines have made work easier and faster to do.

▼ GREENE'S GIN

In the past, men were often given credit for women's ideas. The cotton gin is credited to Eli Whitney in 1793, but supposedly Catherine Greene thought of the invention and even paid Whitney to create it. The cotton gin, which separates cotton fibers from seeds, made it possible for one person to do the work previously performed by 50 people.

MAKING ◀ HAY

Cyrus McCormack's mechanical reaper went on the market in 1841. Using this machine, farmers could harvest 10 to 30 times as much wheat as they could using scythes. The "extravagant Yankee contrivance," as a British paper called it, soon made American agriculture the envy of the world.

▲ RAT–A–TAT

The ancestor of the modern machine gun, known as the Gatling gun, consisted of ten rifles attached to a crank-operated shaft. Invented in 1862, it could fire 350 rounds a minute. The inventor, Dr. Richard Gatling, claimed that his weapon would actually save lives by ending wars sooner.

▲ Steam tractors built in the early 19th century were so heavy they often got stuck in the soil. Henry Ford developed the gasoline-powered tractor in 1907, which he called an "automobile plow."

◀ START YOUR ENGINES

Engines use energy found in fuel to provide motion or do mechanical work. The first horseless road vehicles were huge steam-powered carriages. But with the invention of the internal combustion engine in 1860, it became possible to build smaller, gasoline-driven vehicles.

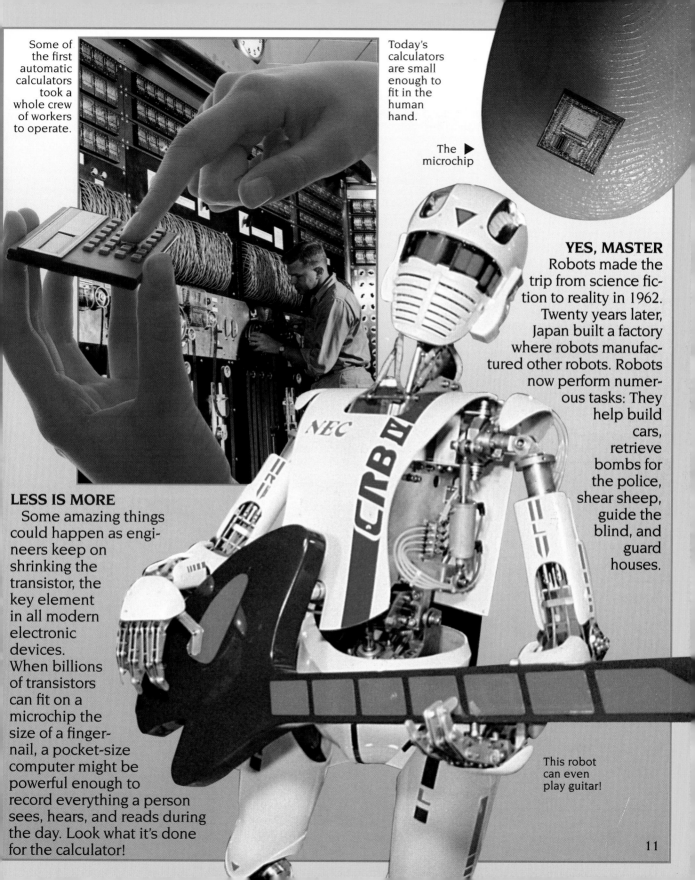

Some of the first automatic calculators took a whole crew of workers to operate.

Today's calculators are small enough to fit in the human hand.

The ▶ microchip

YES, MASTER

Robots made the trip from science fiction to reality in 1962. Twenty years later, Japan built a factory where robots manufactured other robots. Robots now perform numerous tasks: They help build cars, retrieve bombs for the police, shear sheep, guide the blind, and guard houses.

LESS IS MORE

Some amazing things could happen as engineers keep on shrinking the transistor, the key element in all modern electronic devices. When billions of transistors can fit on a microchip the size of a fingernail, a pocket-size computer might be powerful enough to record everything a person sees, hears, and reads during the day. Look what it's done for the calculator!

This robot can even play guitar!

11

Edison invented the alkaline battery.

EVERYDAY ITEMS

People use certain inventions so often, they may not think of these everyday items as extraordinary. But it's hard to imagine life without such things as the clock, the sandwich, or the battery.

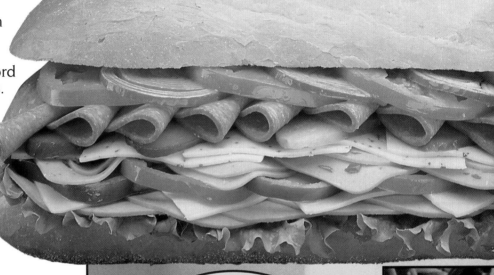

FAST FOOD

Everyone who eats on the run owes a debt to John Montagu (1718–92), an English lord with a passion for cards. When Montagu was gambling nonstop, his cook would bring him two pieces of bread with a slice of meat between them. The snack became popular and was named after Montagu, the 4th Earl of Sandwich.

BOUNCY BOUNCY

What material can hold air, erase pencil marks, and bounce high in the air? Rubber! Long before Columbus arrived, the natives of South America were making shoes and coats with the rubber from rubber trees. Today, we use it to make tires, balloons, sneakers, and thousands of other items. And now we know how to make it synthetically.

WHOOSH!

The first vacuum cleaners were so bulky that most required more than one person to operate them. Vacuum cleaners became so popular in England that people had tea parties where guests would gather to watch the servants do the vacuuming.

ALL SEWED UP

In 1846, Boston's Elias Howe matched his newly invented sewing machine against a team of top–notch seamstresses. Operated by a foot pedal, the machine proved to be five times faster than the best seamstress.

SEEING IS BELIEVING

The ancient Greeks understood the ability of lenses to magnify objects. But eyeglasses did not become possible until the 1290s, when Italian craftspeople discovered how to make clear glass. This invention also made telescopes and microscopes possible.

MARKING TIME

Pope Sylvester II is given credit for inventing the first modern clock in the year 991. Clocks were limited to public spaces until the Italian architect Filippo Brunelleschi invented a portable model in 1410. Pocket–sized clocks came to be called "watches" because they were carried by night watchmen on their rounds.

FANTASTIC PLASTIC

In 1909 the American chemist L. H. Baekeland invented Bakelite, an early form of plastic. By midcentury, this inexpensive and durable material began replacing wood, metal, and glass in the making of countless everyday articles, including toys, bottles, eyeglasses, furniture, and appliances.

Before the invention of plastic, the toothbrush was carved from wood, and its bristles were natural fibers taken from hogs!

STICKY STUFF

Velcro, invented by Swiss engineer Georges de Mestral, is shown here as seen under an electron microscope. On finding thistles stuck to his clothes after a hike, de Mestral examined the thistles and invented the system of hooks and loops that makes Velcro so magically clingy.

ROLLING ALONG

Despite the early invention of the wheel, ground transportation through the ages relied mainly on horses, oxen, and shoe leather. Only with advances in machinery and road building during the 19th century could inventors turn their talents to the job of moving people quickly on the surface of the earth.

◀ At work in 1832, the "Atlantic" was one of the earliest trains.

The TGV ▼

IRON HORSE

The first commercial railroad in the United States was the Baltimore & Ohio, which opened in 1828. The B & O's first steam locomotive, "Tom Thumb," could pull a train at 6 miles per hour. Modern high–speed trains, such as France's TGV, can reach 245 miles per hour.

PEOPLE MOVERS

Streetcars were the first form of mass public transportation, beginning in Paris around 1820 with horse-drawn omnibuses. San Francisco's famous cable cars, run by a steam-driven generator, began to operate in 1873. The first successful electrified streetcar system opened in Richmond, Virginia, in 1888.

An electric streetcar operating in Washington, D.C., in 1895.

ON THE BUS

The highway boom of the 1920s and 1930s made buses a popular form of travel, and by the 1950s they had replaced streetcars as the main form of city transport. School buses came into use during the 1930s, transporting students who lived miles from the nearest school.

PUTT-PUTT

The first successful car with a gasoline engine was built in Germany in 1888 by Gottlieb Daimler and Karl Benz. But American automotive pioneers surged ahead in 1908, when Henry Ford introduced the rugged and affordable Model T—he sold 15 million over the next 20 years.

An electric car

Henry Ford's ▶ first car, called the "Quadricycle," was built in 1896. It weighed 500 pounds and had only two forward speeds.

A solar-powered car

CLEAN MACHINES

Scientists believe that one day cars may run on fuel cells, or batteries, that convert hydrogen and oxygen into electric power. The hydrogen could be produced by solar energy or obtained from biomass (trees and grasses). Unlike gasoline engines, fuel cells would produce no waste, heat, noise, or pollutants.

TWO-WHEELING

Compact and easy to maneuver, the motorcycle is a popular alternative to the automobile, as both a mode of travel and a racing machine. The motorcycle got its start in 1885 when carmaker Gottlieb Daimler placed an engine on a bicycle frame.

15

Many aspiring pilots tried muscle-powered flight—an idea actually patented in 1889 by R. J. Spaulding who, of course, stole it from the birds.

UP, UP, AND AWAY!

Since ancient times, human beings dreamed of soaring like birds. Numerous flying machines were built during the 19th and early 20th centuries. However, until the Wright Brothers came along, no one ever managed to fly a powered machine and bring it down without crashing.

QUIET CONQUEST

On December 17, 1903, when Wilbur and Orville Wright's Flyer made history at Kitty Hawk, North Carolina, hardly anyone knew about it. The public had become so doubtful about flying machines that only three newspapers bothered to report the event.

BALLOONING

Before there were planes, people traveled high in the sky in balloons. The first flights were made in the late 18th century in France. Although used by the military for observation during World War I, the balloon never became an important mode of transportation. However, people enjoy sport ballooning even today.

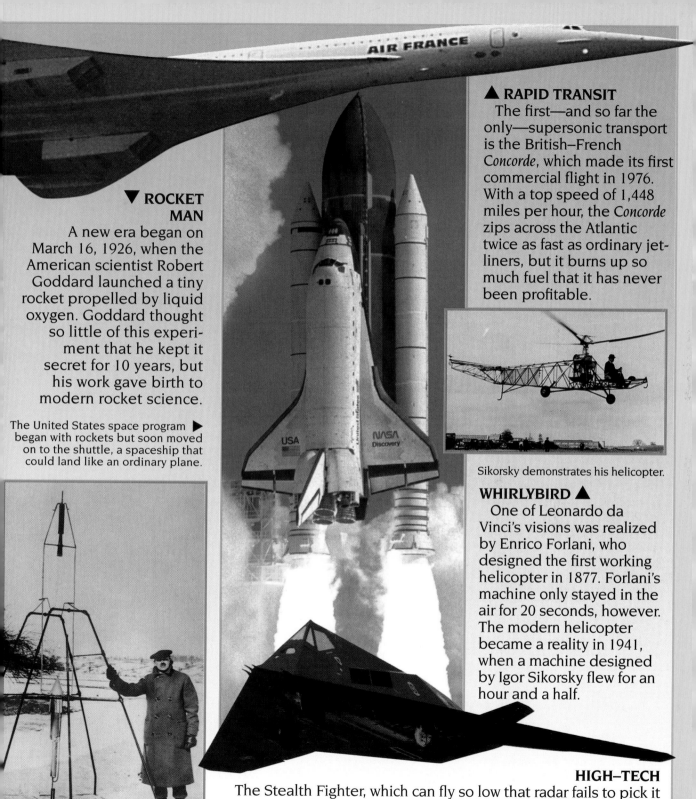

▲ RAPID TRANSIT

The first—and so far the only—supersonic transport is the British–French *Concorde*, which made its first commercial flight in 1976. With a top speed of 1,448 miles per hour, the *Concorde* zips across the Atlantic twice as fast as ordinary jetliners, but it burns up so much fuel that it has never been profitable.

▼ ROCKET MAN

A new era began on March 16, 1926, when the American scientist Robert Goddard launched a tiny rocket propelled by liquid oxygen. Goddard thought so little of this experiment that he kept it secret for 10 years, but his work gave birth to modern rocket science.

The United States space program ▶ began with rockets but soon moved on to the shuttle, a spaceship that could land like an ordinary plane.

Sikorsky demonstrates his helicopter.

WHIRLYBIRD ▲

One of Leonardo da Vinci's visions was realized by Enrico Forlani, who designed the first working helicopter in 1877. Forlani's machine only stayed in the air for 20 seconds, however. The modern helicopter became a reality in 1941, when a machine designed by Igor Sikorsky flew for an hour and a half.

HIGH–TECH

The Stealth Fighter, which can fly so low that radar fails to pick it up, is one of the weapons that will make up the arsenal of the 21st century. Others include bombs and missiles that will be guided to their targets by lasers, optical processors, and space satellites.

WATERWORLD

The first boats date back to prehistoric times, when people hollowed out large tree trunks to make canoes. The ancient Egyptians made the first great advances in water transport. They invented sails in about 3200 B.C.

ROW, ROW, ROW

Around the 6th century B.C., the Greeks began to build *triremes*, large boats propelled by 75 oarsmen. These vessels could travel around 9.5 knots, or about 11 miles per hour.

WHICH WAY'S NORTH?

Today's ships use satellites to pinpoint their location on Earth, but for centuries travelers had only the sun and stars as navigational guides. With the invention of the magnetic compass about 1,000 years ago by the Chinese, traveling became more certain.

In use since the 17th century, the sextant (above) gives a measurement of the angle between two objects in the sky, from which the position of a ship can be calculated.

Commercial sailing ships were competitive well into the age of steam. Today's sailing vessels, such as this tall ship, are used mostly for pleasure or sport.

"FULTON'S FOLLY"

Robert Fulton's first steamboat looked like a sure loser when he launched it in 1807. On its maiden voyage up the Hudson River, the *Clermont* failed to attract a paying passenger and terrified local residents with its smoke, noise, and sparks. Within a short time, however, steamboats dominated the nation's waterways.

BRANCHING OUT

During the 15th century, European voyages to far–off lands—such as Africa and the Americas—were aided by the invention of a new type of sailing ship, the caravel. Lighter and more maneuverable than standard vessels, caravels could navigate narrow passages and sail efficiently into the wind.

FLATTOP

The idea of the aircraft carrier was born in 1911 when Eugene Ely used a platform on the U.S. battleship *Pennsylvania* to take off and land in a Curtiss biplane. In 1925, the U.S. Navy built its first true carrier, USS *Saratoga*, which fought many battles in the Pacific during World War II.

DOWN UNDER

The first U.S. submarine, known as the *Turtle*, was built by David Bushnell in 1776 for use in the Revolutionary War. Made of wood with glass windows, the *Turtle* had room for one person, a 30–minute air supply, and a top speed of 3 miles per hour. Almost two centuries later, in 1958, the first nuclear–powered submarine, the USS *Nautilus*, crossed the icy Arctic Ocean.

The *Queen Elizabeth* luxury liner

Combining pedal power with ingenuity, this inventor has created a new way to navigate the waterways.

OCEAN LUXURY

The age of glamorous shipboard travel began in 1897, when Germany launched the first modern luxury liner, *Kaiser Wilhelm der Grosse* (King William the Great). This floating hotel could carry more than 2,000 passengers.

HELLO!

The challenge of finding new ways to widen the range of human contact has inspired some of the world's greatest inventors. As a result, the world has become a smaller and smaller place as communications have improved.

PAPER TRAIL

Paper dates back to ancient Egypt, when scribes made papyrus out of reeds. Modern paper was invented in China around A.D. 105 by T'sai Lun, who mixed mulberry bark, hemp, and cloth with water, pressed the pulp into sheets, and hung them out to dry.

PEN TO PAPER

The use of quill pens dates back nearly 5,000 years to ancient Egypt. Lewis E. Waterman, an insurance broker, patented the first successful fountain pen in 1884. He soon gave up insurance and went into the pen business.

PRINT IT! ▲

The Chinese invented movable type, placing individual letters on single blocks. The modern printing press was born in the 1420s when Germany's Johann Gutenberg devised a way to make movable type quickly and cheaply. Thanks to him, the average person—not just the rich—finally had access to books.

CLICKETY–CLACK

Philo Remington patented his first typewriter in 1873, but the device was a flop until the 1880s, when he increased its potential speed to 90 words a minute. Businessmen then began to buy the machines and hire typists, bringing women into the office for the first time.

GOING GLOBAL

In 1895, Guglielmo Marconi transmitted radio signals. This new technology made wireless communication possible. In 1960, the United States launched *Echo*, a space satellite that captured radio signals and redirected them back to Earth. International telephone calls were suddenly faster, cheaper, and of a better quality.

FAMOUS FIRST WORDS ▲

In 1876, Alexander Graham Bell perfected a device for transmitting sound waves across electrical wires. The very first telephone communication was Bell's summons to his assistant: "Mr. Watson, come here—I want you."

HEAT'S ON ▲

In 1944, Carl Miller devised a technique of reproducing images on heat–sensitive paper through the use of infrared rays. From his work, came the facsimile, or fax machine.

During World War II, radio communication enabled armies to coordinate their movements.

This enterprising eleven-year-old invented an underwater walkie-talkie.

21

THAT'S ENTERTAINMENT!

Until the 20th century, people gathered at dances, concerts, and festivals for their entertainment. With advances in technology, we can now see and hear in our home almost anything we like with the click of a button.

An early phonograph

FANCY PICKIN'

Around 1930, the Dopyera brothers created the Dobro, a guitar equipped with a device that transmitted vibrations to an amplifier. The first modern electric guitar *pickup* was patented by Leo Fender in the 1940s and became the basis for the legendary Fender Stratocaster.

The microphone, invented by Edison, and the guitar give Sting the technological edge he needs to rock 'n' roll.

TALKING MACHINE

Thomas Edison's first phonograph, invented in 1877, played grooved metal cylinders covered with tinfoil. When reporters visited Edison's lab, the machine welcomed them, asked about their health, wondered how they liked the phonograph, and then said good-night.

In the 1950s, the jukebox (above), a kind of musical vending machine, offered a wide selection of favorite tunes, playing any grooved album selected.

ON THE RADIO

With the invention of radio communication, a new entertainment was born. Throughout the 1930s and 1940s, the radio captivated the whole family, in much the same way as television does today—with news, comedy, sports, and more.

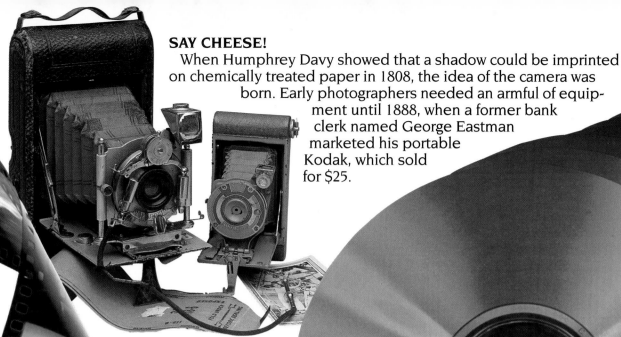

SAY CHEESE!

When Humphrey Davy showed that a shadow could be imprinted on chemically treated paper in 1808, the idea of the camera was born. Early photographers needed an armful of equipment until 1888, when a former bank clerk named George Eastman marketed his portable Kodak, which sold for $25.

SOUND TO GO

The five–inch compact disk (CD) was developed in 1979 by two electronics giants, Philips and Sony. Within a few years, the CD drove vinyl records out of the stores.

ROLL 'EM!

Using film supplied by Eastman, Thomas Edison invented the first high–speed moving picture camera, the Kinetoscope, in 1893. The Kinetoscope could record 46 frames a second on a 50–foot band of film. Spectators could watch movies by peering into a box through a small glass slot.

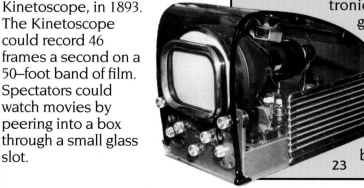

UNSUNG HERO ▼

Philo T. Farnsworth, a 14–year–old Idaho farm boy, came up with the idea for electronic television in 1921 and gave the first public TV demonstration in 1934. But the giant RCA Corporation won the race to manufacture a commercial TV set, and Farnsworth's genius has only recently been recognized.

▲ This invention combines picture and sound in a portable player.

FUN AND GAMES

Toys and games have existed since the beginning of human society. Children made their own dolls out of wood and clay in prehistoric times. Some games—such as cat's cradle—have been played for centuries.

BARBIE FOREVER

The Greeks and Romans had dolls with movable limbs, and European dolls had clothing centuries ago. But no doll in history has had as much fun as Barbie. Since her creation in 1958, Barbie has acquired an outfit for every occasion, a handsome boyfriend, and her own computer.

Thomas Edison invented the first talking doll around 1888. A miniature phonograph inside provided sound.

◀ Popular in the 1870s, the Penny Farthing wasn't chain-driven, but its large wheel provided speed.

BIG WHEELS

The modern bicycle hit the market in the 1880s, and cycling soon became a craze in Europe and the United States. Before they ever flew a plane, Orville and Wilbur Wright made a name for themselves by manufacturing America's most affordable bicycles.

FLYING SAUCER

During the 1950s, students at Yale University loved the pies made by the Frisbie Bakery in Bridgeport, Connecticut. After eating their fill they would play catch with the tinfoil pie plates. This inspired a California company named Wham–O to make plastic disks with a curved edge, and the Frisbee was born.

UP AND DOWN

A toy with a history, the yo-yo originated in China about 2,500 years ago, and was introduced to the United States in 1929. Used as a weapon in the 16th century by Philippine jungle fighters, the yo-yo is today a toy with lots of play value. Real tricksters can make a yo-yo do the spinner, the forward pass, the breakaway, and the creeper.

n-ine kates ave rotten a ew nventive boost from his young woman. She has designed a device that allows skaters to walk on non-skatable surfaces without removing their skates.

GREAT SKATES

In 1759 Joseph Merlin made a grand impression when he zipped into a London ballroom on home-made two–wheel roller skates, playing the violin—and promptly crashed into a wall. Despite his nasty accident skating became popular, and in 1863 James L. Plimpton of New York invented a safer roller skate with four wheels.

◄ Not able to use his hands for playing video games, this young inventor has created a device that allows him to use his head.

NEW WAY TO PLAY

The first computer game, Pong (1972), was an electronic tennis match that was pretty tame by today's standards. The first of the high–energy games was Space Invaders, introduced in 1978 by Taito of Japan. In Space Invaders, the player took on a host of warlike Martians.

ROUNDBALL

In 1891, YMCA instructor James Naismith invented basketball in Springfield, Massachusetts, as a way of keeping athletes in shape during the winter. The first games were played with a soccer ball and a pair of peach baskets.

MAKING IT BETTER

Even the doctors of the ancient world, who did not understand the causes of disease, developed remarkable skills in treating ailments and healing wounds. Today, from replaceable organs to gene therapy, science is inventing new ways to deal with illness.

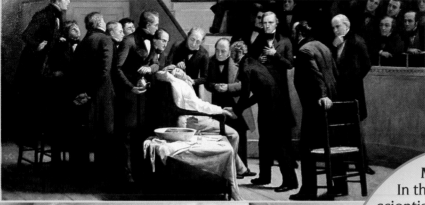

FEELING NO PAIN

Before anesthesia, patients had to "bite the bullet" during an operation. Surgery took a major step forward in 1842, when Crawford W. Long used ether to render a patient unconscious during a tooth extraction. The new technique caught on quickly after England's Queen Victoria underwent anesthesia to ease the pain of childbirth.

◀ The first public demonstration of surgery with anesthesia took place in 1848 in Massachusetts General Hospital.

IN THE DARK ▼

One of medicine's most valuable tools, the X ray, was discovered by accident in 1895, by Wilhelm Roentgen. He called the mysterious radiation the X ray because he had no idea what it was.

MAGIC PILLS

In the 1890s, German scientist Felix Hoffman was searching for a way to help his father, who was suffering from arthritis. After studying some forgotten 50–year–old experiments on the pain–relieving powers of salicylic acid, Hoffman developed aspirin, which became the world's most popular painkiller.

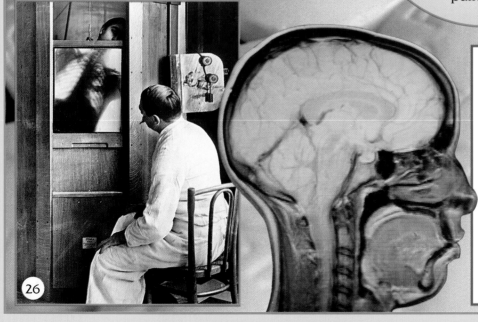

ADDED DIMENSIONS

Though X rays revolutionized medicine, they had one limitation—all the images they provided were two–dimensional. In 1972, researchers came up with computerized axial tomographic scanning—the CAT scan—which combines a number of X ray pictures into a three–dimensional image.

ZOOM IN ▼

Looking through an ordinary magnifying glass, a person can see an object enlarged up to 15 diameters, or 15x. That's nothing compared to the power of the electron microscope, which can magnify objects up to about 500,000x.

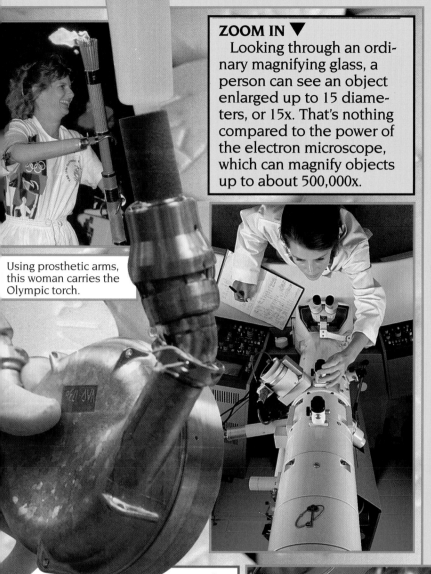

Using prosthetic arms, this woman carries the Olympic torch.

AMAZING LASERS

Among their many other applications, lasers have become surgical instruments. These powerful beams of light cut through flesh and seal off blood vessels.

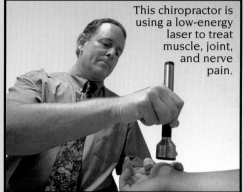

This chiropractor is using a low-energy laser to treat muscle, joint, and nerve pain.

HIGH-TECH SURGERY ▼

With the invention of better equipment, surgery has vastly improved in the last century. One of medicine's future wonders involves a temporary replacement for human blood that would allow surgeons to place a patient in near-freezing temperatures. Surgeons could then stop the heart for several hours to perform complicated operations.

◀ A mechanical heart

NEW PARTS

Even since ancient times artificial limbs have been in use. One of history's most celebrated artificial parts was built in 1509 for a knight. This three-pound hand had movable fingers with which the knight could grasp his sword. Today, not only are *limbs* being replaced, there are also artificial organs, such as the heart and skin, blood vessels, noses and ears.

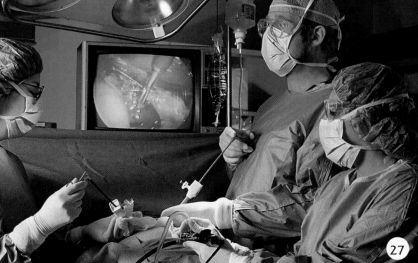

COMPUTER WORLD

The computer has catapulted the world into a new era, where almost all aspects of life—from communications and industry to cinema and every field of science—virtually depend upon this 20th century invention.

SMART MACHINE ▲

The first mainframe computer, known as ENIAC (Electronic Numeric Integrator and Calculator), was unveiled in 1945. It weighed over 30 tons and filled an entire room. In its first official test, ENIAC spent two hours completing a complex nuclear physics calculation—the same task would have occupied 100 engineers for a full year.

LITTLE CHIP

Smaller and smaller computers came about as technology developed, first with the use of the transistor in the late 1950s, and then with the invention of the silicon chip, which could hold many transistors. The silicon chip and transistor brought about the microprocessor, the first computer circuit to fit on a single chip. From this boom in technology came the personal computer, or PC, first sold in 1975.

▼ A laptop PC

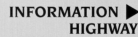

INFORMATION ▶ HIGHWAY

Though the Internet became the hot medium of the 1990s, it actually began in the early 1960s. Known as ARPAnet, it linked the computers of scientists working on U.S. Defense Department projects.

VIRTUAL FLIGHT ▲

Able to generate the virtual experience of flying, computers can provide a pilot many hours of training on the ground. In emergency situations simulated by the computer, the pilot can learn from his or her mistakes without putting a crew in danger. Pilots can crash and learn, rather than crash and burn.

SPORT OF KINGS

The earliest recorded chess games were played in Persia around the year 500. The term checkmate comes from *sháh mát*, a Persian phrase meaning "the king cannot escape." What's happening to that game today? It's being mastered by a computer known as Deep Blue. A current goal in technology is to develop true artificial intelligence, in which a machine can solve problems in creative ways.

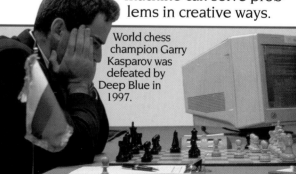

World chess champion Garry Kasparov was defeated by Deep Blue in 1997.

◀ GET REAL

Virtual Reality (VR) is an interactive computer technology that launches people into three–dimensional cyberspace. It began in the 1970s with experiments at the Massachusetts Institute of Technology. By the 1980s, the Atari Corporation had VR ready for fun and games.

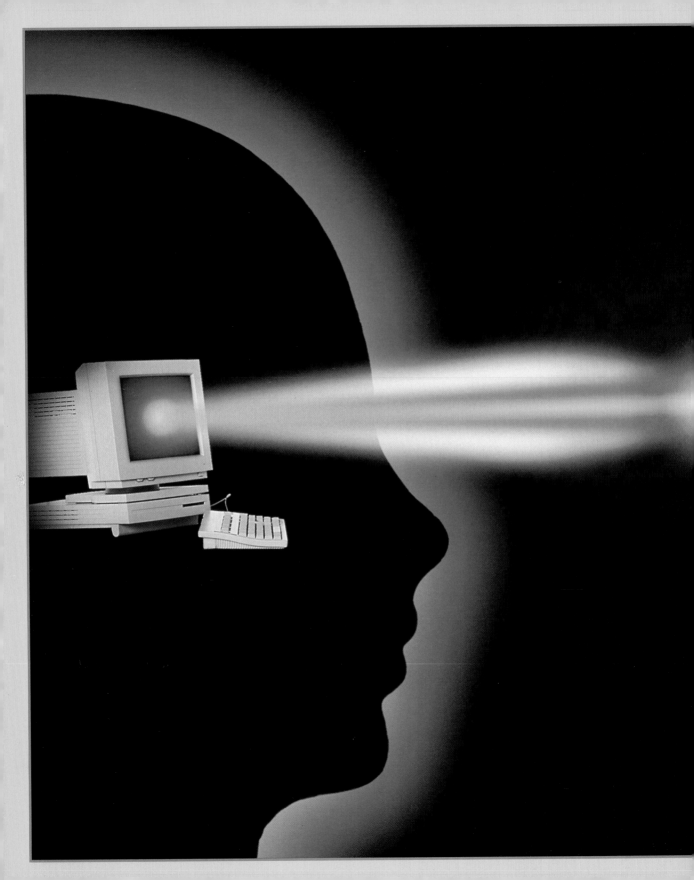

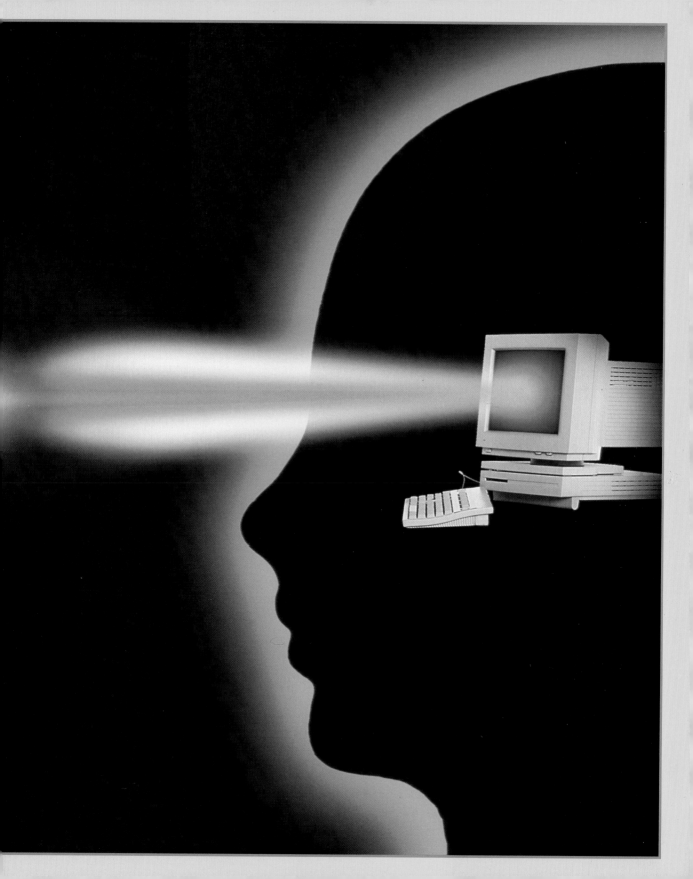